WHAT MAKES A PLANT A PLANT?

STRUCTURE AND DEFENSES

SCIENCE BOOK FOR CHILDREN
Children's Science & Nature Books

BABY PROFESSOR
EDUCATION KIDS

Speedy Publishing LLC
40 E. Main St. #1156
Newark, DE 19711
www.speedypublishing.com

Plants are live organisms covering much of the land on Earth and are seen everywhere. They are a part of the kingdom plantae and include trees, grasses, bushes, flowers, mosses, ferns, and more. In this book, you will be learning about their structure and their defenses.

WHAT MAKES IT A PLANT?

Echeveria Succulent Plant.

Basil Plant.

Some of the basic characteristics that make it a plant are listed here:

- Most of them use a process known as photosynthesis to make their food.

- They have a cuticle, which means there is a waxy layer on top of their surface to protect them and keep them from becoming too dry.

- They have what is known as eukaryotic cells that have cell walls that are rigid.

- They use either spore or sex cells for reproduction.

WHAT IS A PLANT CELL?

They are composed of the rigid cells walls that are made from cellulose, chloroplasts that help with the photosynthesis process, the nucleus, and the large vacuoles that are filled with water.

They are a type of eukaryotic cell found in plants. These cells are different than other types of eukaryotic cells since the organelles are different and organelles are the key part of a cell.

LIGHT REACTION & CALVIN CYCLE

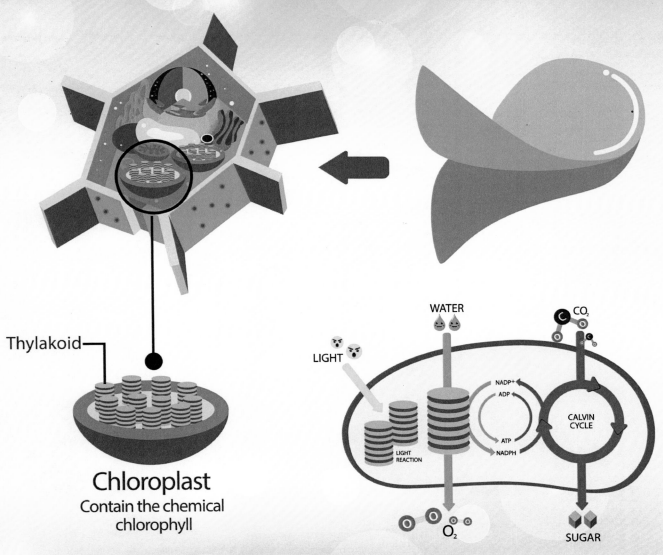

Thylakoid

Chloroplast
Contain the chemical chlorophyll

WATER

CO₂

LIGHT

NADP+

ADP

ATP

NADPH

LIGHT REACTION

CALVIN CYCLE

O₂

SUGAR

Photosynthesis plant cell diagram.

Photosynthesis is a process used by plants.

The one big difference is that the plant cell has a rigid cell wall surrounding the cell membrane. Other types of organisms have cell walls surrounding their cells, but the cell walls in plants contain cellulose and protein. This cell wall protects the cell and provides the plant with its structure and shape.

Secondly, these cells contain chlorophyll which makes the plant green in color and also assists with the photosynthesis process which they utilize in making their own food using water, sunlight and carbon dioxide.

Lastly, they have large central vacuoles which are in some of the other eukaryotes, but in plants cells they are larger structures. The vacuoles are a space for holding materials which the plant may need or may not need, including water, food and waste.

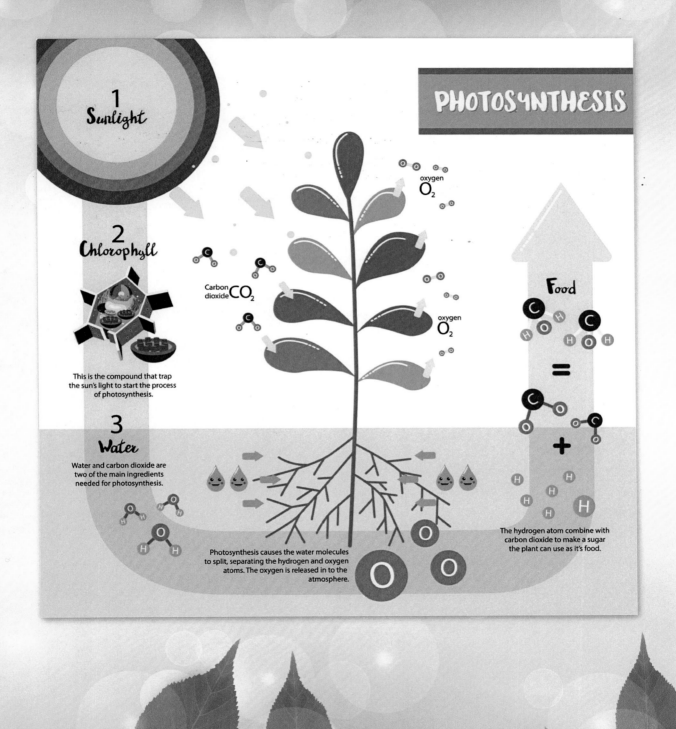

THE SUN'S ENERGY

Photosynthesis is one of the key functions of most plants. They use it to make energy directly from the sunlight.

DIFFERENT TYPES OF PLANTS

There are many different species of plants and typically, they are divided into these two key groups: vascular and nonvascular.

- **VASCULAR PLANTS** have tissues that help in moving materials like water throughout it. They can be divided further into flowering and non-flowing plants. Plants such as flowers, trees, and bushes are some of the organisms that fit into this group.

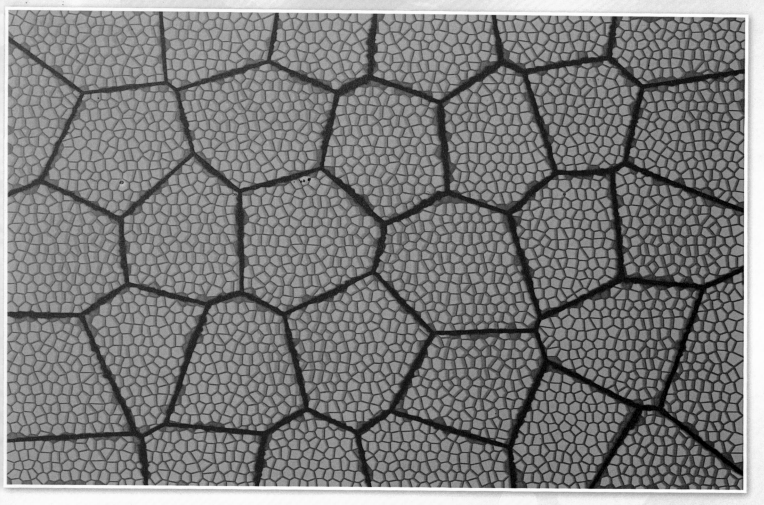

Vascular Structure of a Leaf.

- **NONVASCULAR** are plants like mosses, which are smaller, and use osmosis and diffusion to move the necessary materials throughout it.

Moss

BASIC STRUCTURE OF PLANTS

The leaf, stem, and roots are the three standard parts of most types of vascular plants.

- **THE LEAF** is considered as a plant's organ specialized for the photosynthesis process. They obtain energy from the sunlight and collect carbon dioxide from the air. Several leaves are thin and flat so they are able to get as much sunlight as they can.

They do however come in several different shapes, including the skinny long needles found on pine trees.

- The main structure supporting the leaves and flowers is **THE STEM**. They have vascular tissues for moving water and food throughout the plant to assist with its growth. Food for the plants in often stored in the stems.

- The plant's **ROOTS** grow underneath the ground and help to protect it from falling over as well as gather minerals and water from the soil. There are some plant species that store food in the roots. There are two key types of roots; taproots and fibrous roots. Fibrous roots have several roots growing in all different directions and taproots more than likely will have a major one that goes very deep.

Sprout of oak with root in ground.

THE PLANT DEFENSES

From the largest mammal to the smallest insect, most animals eat plants for food. They are known as herbivores. You may believe that they just lay on the ground and get eaten since they are not able to move. However, they have many defenses they use for survival.

WHAT ARE THE TWO TYPES OF DEFENSES

Plants have two key types of defenses known as constitutive and induced.

- The constitutive defense is always present in a plant. Most defenses are constitutive.

- The induced defense is a short-term defense targeted to defend an area of the plant that has been injured or attacked.

Resin on Injured Tree.

LEAF ANATOMY

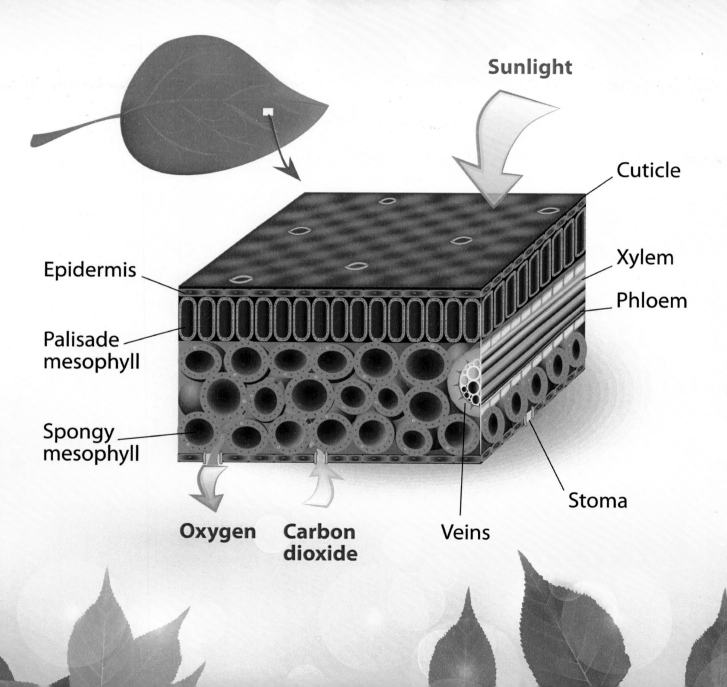

Sunlight

Cuticle

Xylem

Phloem

Epidermis

Palisade mesophyll

Spongy mesophyll

Oxygen

Carbon dioxide

Veins

Stoma

WHAT ARE CELL WALLS AND CUTICLES?

Similar to humans, plants are susceptible to diseases that make them ill and die. To be able to keep the small bacteria and pathogens from getting inside of it, they have firm cell walls. The leaves have a waxy cuticle to protect them.

WHAT DOES THE BARK DO?

They also need a defense against insects. The branches on many species of bushes and trees have a thick bark on them to keep out any insects. This bark contains several layers and the outside of it is hard and dead. This bark will keep all but the most determined bugs from finding a way to get in the tree's trunk.

Pine Forest

Cactus Close-up

THORNS

Thorns are used by some plants as protection from being eaten by a larger animal. They are able to poke and bother the animal bad enough that it will move on to a different plant. Examples of thorns are the cactus spines and the roses on the stem of a rose. Some types of cactus spines are more dangerous since they have barbs that will stick in your skin and is not easily removed.

CHEMICAL DEFENSES

Plants will often develop a chemical that works like a poison and make the animal sick or even might kill it. Animals learn over time which plants are poisonous and will stay away from them. These include chrysanthemums, daffodil bulbs, foxglove, wisteria and poison ivy.

Chrysanthemums

Poison Ivy

BAD TASTE

Many plants use chemicals which give them a bitter taste to keep from being eaten. An animal will move on to a better tasting plant.

CARNIVOROUS PLANTS

There are some types of plants that can not only defend against insects, they can eat them. The venus flytrap is one such example. When a fly, or other type of insect, lands on its leaves, it will snap the trap quickly, which releases enzymes to help it to digest the insect it just caught.

Venus Fly Trap.

Tulip Field

FLOWERING PLANTS

Flowering plants produce flowers for reproduction. They produce seeds which are inside the fruit of the plant. Angiosperms is their scientific name.

FRUITS

Many plants distribute their seeds by their fruits. After the flower has been fertilized with pollen, the fruits are formed. The flower transforms into fruit once the ovules in the pistil have become seeds.

SEEDS

The embryo of the plant is the seed, similar to a baby plant. Depending on what type of plant it is, the seeds come in various colors and shapes. Inside of this seed is the embryo of the plant, food to sustain the embryo, and the seed coat for protection.

Jojoba Seeds

WHAT IS POLLINATION?

An ovary must receive pollen in order for it to become a seed. Birds and insects play a major role in plant pollination. When a bird or an insect is drawn to a flower because of its bright color, pollen gets on them. Moving from one plant to another they transfer the pollen from plant to plant. This process helps them reproduce by creation of the seeds.

Pollen grain flying from birch tree catkins.

NON-FLOWERING PLANTS

Ficus Plant.

NON-FLOWERING PLANTS DO NOT USE FLOWERS FOR REPRODUCTION. WHAT IS POLLINATION?

There are two key groups of non-flowering plants, the type that use spores for reproduction and the ones that use seeds for reproduction. The group that uses seeds are known as gymnosperms.

An Ornamental Gymnosperm plant.

GYMNOSPERMS

The word gymnosperm means *"naked seeds"*. They get this name since the seeds are open in the air and have no covering like seeds of the flowering plants. The conifer is one of the gymnosperm key groups.

CONIFERS

The term *"conifers"* means *"bearing cones"*. These plants use cones for housing their seeds. They are woody plants and mostly trees like Firs, Cypresses, Pine Trees, Cedars, Junipers and Redwoods.

Branches of a Fir Tree

CONES

Conifers use their cones for reproduction. Some of them are female, and some are male. The cones that are male release the pollen, which is then carried by the wind. If it lands on a female cone, the female will then produce seeds. The cone has hard scales that protect the new seeds.

Pine Cones

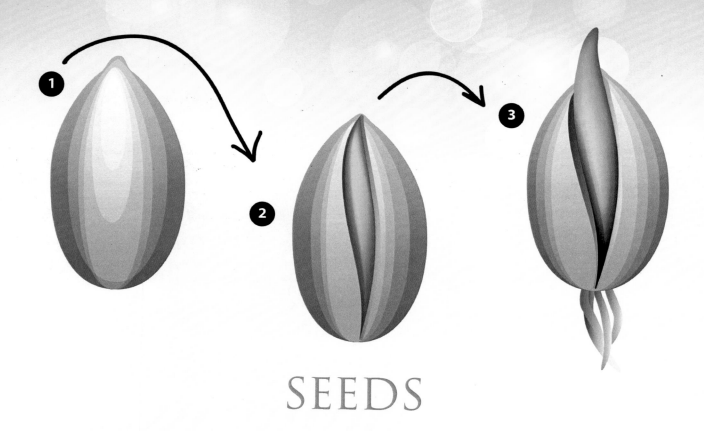

SEEDS

The conifer's seeds are winged. Once the cone releases them, they are able to float with the wind until they hit the ground where they germinate and grow.

SPORES

Some non-flowering plants do not produce seeds, but use spores for reproduction. Mosses and ferns are just a couple types of spore producing plants.

The next time you are outside, take a look at the plants around you and think about their structure and how they defend themselves, as well as whether they are a flowering or non-flowering plant.

For additional information about plant structure and defenses, you can go to your local library, research the internet, and ask questions of your teachers, family and friends.

Cones and leaves of Deodar or Himalayan Cedar (Cedrus deodara).

Visit

BABY PROFESSOR
EDUCATION KIDS

www.BabyProfessorBooks.com

to download Free Baby Professor eBooks
and view our catalog of new and exciting
Children's Books

Made in the USA
San Bernardino, CA
20 August 2018